# More! Instant Bible Lessons

## Jesus' Disciples

Pamela J. Kuhn

**These pages may be copied.**

Permission is granted to the buyer of this book to photocopy student materials in this book for use with Sunday school or Bible teaching classes.

Rainbow Publishers

Rainbow Publishers • P.O. Box 261129 • San Diego, CA 92196
www.rainbowpublishers.com

Dedicated to Jordan Satterfield who, like the twelve, has heard and responded to the call of Jesus.

MORE! INSTANT BIBLE LESSONS: JESUS' DISCIPLES
©2009 by Rainbow Publishers, ninth printing
ISBN 10: 1-58411-017-1
ISBN 13: 978-1-58411-017-0
Rainbow reorder# RB36625
RELIGION/Christian Ministry/Children

Rainbow Publishers
P.O. Box 261129
San Diego, CA 92196
www.rainbowpublishers.com

Cover illustrator: Terry Julien
Interior illustrator: Chuck Galey

SUSTAINABLE FORESTRY INITIATIVE

Certified Chain of Custody
Promoting Sustainable
Forest Management
www.sfiprogram.org

*Printed in the United States of America*

# Contents

# Introduction

What were the men who were closest to Jesus really like? Did you know Thomas was a twin, that Judas often took money from the disciples' treasury to increase his own riches or that one of the disciples was called three different names? You'll find the answers to these questions as you study the lessons in *Jesus' Disciples*.

Each of the first eight chapters includes a Bible story, memory verse and numerous activities to help reinforce the lessons about the disciples. An additional chapter contains projects about the rarely mentioned disciples. Teacher aides are also sprinkled throughout the book, including bulletin board ideas and discussion starters.

As you work through the lessons, you may use your own judgment as to the appropriateness of the projects for your class. Everything in this book is designed to meet the interests and abilities of the 5 to 10 age range, however some activities may be more appealing to a younger group while others will more readily meet the abilities of older children.

The most exciting aspect of the *Instant Bible Lessons* series is its flexibility. You can easily adapt these lessons to a Sunday School hour, a children's church service, a Wednesday night Bible study, Christian school classroom or family home use. And, because there is a variety of reproducible ideas from which to choose, you will enjoy creating a class session that is best for your group of students — whether large or small, beginning or advanced, active or studious.

This book is written to add fun and uniqueness to learning about the men closest to Jesus. Teaching children is exciting and rewarding, especially when you are successful in hiding God's Word and its principles in the hearts of your students. *Instant Bible Lessons* will help you accomplish that goal. Blessings on you as your class learns how to become disciples of Jesus.

## How to Use This Book

Each chapter begins with a Bible story for you to read to your class, followed by discussion questions. Then, use any or all of the activities in the chapter to help drive home the message of that lesson. All of the activities are tagged with one of the icons below, so you can quickly flip through the chapter and select the projects you need. Simply cut off the teacher instructions on the pages and duplicate as desired.

| craft | skit | teacher help | bulletin board | activity |
|---|---|---|---|---|
| puzzle | action song | song | game | snack |

# Chapter 1
# Andrew, Sharer of Christ

## Memory Verse

*Those who lead many to righteousness [will shine] like the stars for ever and ever.* Daniel 12:3

## Story to Share
## I Have Found the Messiah!

John the Baptist preached about the One who would come. "One is coming who is greater than I am. Follow Him. He is the Son of God."

John the Baptist had many followers. As he preached about Jesus, many believed and were baptized.

Andrew, one of John the Baptist's followers, was walking with his brother, Simon Peter (later known as simply "Peter"), and with John the Baptist. Jesus was walking past. John said, "Look! The Lamb of God."

Andrew's heart warmed as he looked at the man called Jesus. Speaking to John, he said, "John, my heart was warmed just to look at Jesus."

"Andrew," said John, "you should go and follow Jesus."

Andrew obeyed, following behind Jesus. When Jesus realized someone was behind Him, He turned around and said, "What do you want?"

Andrew looked into the kind eyes of Jesus and answered, "I would like to know where You are staying. I would like to listen to You teach."

"Come," said Jesus. "You'll see where I am staying."

What a wonderful day Andrew had listening to the teachings of Jesus. He was so excited! He could hardly wait to tell someone else about what he had learned. He didn't want to hide this Good News about the Messiah — he wanted to share it. "I want to tell everyone I meet that I have found the man John has been telling us about."

Finding his brother, Andrew said, "Simon, Simon, I have found the Messiah. Come on and let me take you to Him."

Andrew brought his brother to Jesus and Simon Peter also followed Jesus.

— based on John 1:35-51

## Discussion Questions

1. Who first told Andrew about Jesus? (John the Baptist)
2. What did Andrew do when he followed Jesus? (brought his brother back to Jesus)

## puzzle

### What You Need
- duplicated page
- 3 different crayons

### What to Do
1. Give each child a duplicated page and three different crayons.
2. Read the instructions aloud and explain what to do. The answer key is on page 93.

### What to Say
What do we call someone who brings others to Jesus? (an evangelist) Andrew was the first evangelist. He brought his brother to Jesus. Home is always a good place to start to tell others about Jesus.

**ANDREW**

# Back and Forth

Use your first crayon to draw a path for Andrew to go to Jesus. Use your second crayon to draw a different path for Andrew to run back to tell Peter about Jesus. Use your third crayon to find a different path for Andrew to take Peter to Jesus.

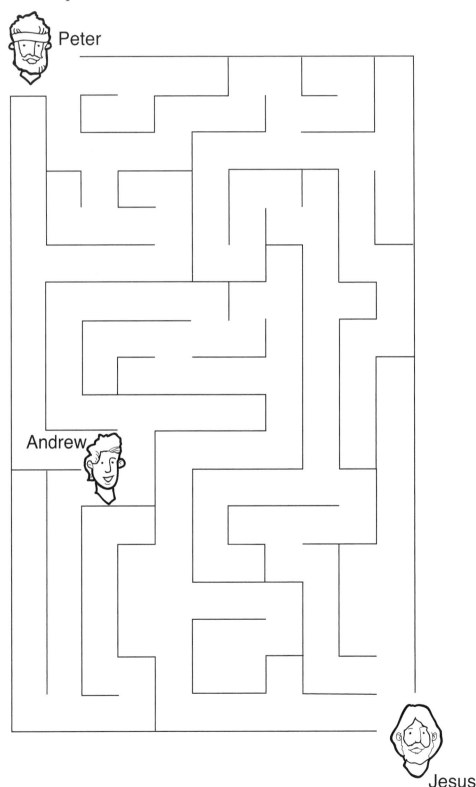

# Happy with Second Place

### What You Need

- duplicated page
- glue
- scissors
- small paper plates
- crayons
- markers

### What to Do

1. Have the students cut out the circle and glue it to a paper plate.
2. Instruct them to choose a partner.
3. Stand 8 feet from the students. At the start signal, the first two should put their paper plates on their heads and walk toward you. They may not touch the plate. If the plate falls off, they must start over.
4. The first one to make it to you gets a #1 on his or her trophy. The next one gets a #2.
5. Continue until all pairs have raced.
6. If you have extra time, the students may color their plates.

## What To Say

(Have all of the number one group sit on one side of you; the number two group on the other.) How did it make you feel to be number one? Number two? Andrew knew Jesus first but when he brought his brother Peter to Him, Peter became closer to Jesus. Yet Andrew had no jealousy in his heart about being number two. What does 1 Corinthians 13:4 say? (Allow the students to look up the Scripture: "Love…does not envy.") When you play a game do you want to win the trophy for 1st place or 2nd place? (Continue to use these groups throughout the class: Number one group may serve the number two group the snack first, number one group may line up first, number two group may clean up after the craft, etc.)

**ANDREW**

# Here, Jesus

Use your Bible to finish the story of Andrew and the hungry crowd.

## Andrew and the Hungry Crowd
## John 6:1-13

**What You Need**
- duplicated page
- Bibles
- pencils

**What to Do**
1. Give each child a duplicated page, a Bible and a pencil.
2. Encourage the children to fill in the story by memory and then by looking up the Scripture.
3. The answers are on page 93.

Jesus was tired. He needed a rest so He went to the far shore of the _____. When the crowds heard where He had gone, they _____ Jesus. When Jesus saw the crowd, He felt sorry for them, healed their sick and taught them about God, the Father.

It was getting late. The crowd was hungry. The disciples wanted Jesus to send the people away. Jesus asked, "Where can we buy food for all these people?"

Philip spoke up. It would take _____ months' wages to buy food for this many people to even have a _____.

But Andrew had been busy going through the crowd, trying to find someone who had some food. "Here, Jesus, is a _____ with _____ small barley loaves and _____ small fish."

Jesus asked the disciples to have the people sit on the grassy ground. Jesus gave _____, then had the disciples give the people bread and fish to eat. When everyone had all they could eat, the disciples gathered up the remains. The leftovers filled _____ baskets.

**ANDREW**

# I Have Found Him

## Characters

- John the Baptist
- Jesus
- Andrew
- Peter

## Skit

**John the Baptist:** preaching

**Andrew:** kneeling

**John the Baptist, Andrew and Peter:** walking

**Jesus:** passing the three men

**Andrew:** looking at John, rubbing his heart

**John:** pointing to Jesus

**Andrew:** following Jesus

**Jesus:** preaching

**Andrew:** clapping hands, racing towards Peter, and "talking" excitedly; point to Jesus and gesture, "Come."

**Andrew and Peter:** kneeling in front of Jesus

## John the Baptist

## Andrew

### skit

#### What You Need

- name cards
- poster board
- hole punch
- scissors
- yarn

#### What to Do

1. Duplicate the cards on pages 11 and 12 on poster board.
2. Cut out the cards and punch holes in the black dots.
3. Thread enough yarn through the holes to make a necklace and tie the ends together.
4. Choose four students to pantomime the story.
5. Most of the students in your class will want to participate in the pantomime. Plan time to do it more than once.
6. Keep a box filled with bathrobes, towels, belts, etc., in your room for when your students are acting out the story. Wrap a turban around your head to make a Bible story more interesting!

**ANDREW**

# Jesus

# John

# Loaves and Fishes

## Good Food to Eat

Jesus gives me food to eat.
Sometimes sour, sometimes sweet.
I am thankful for it all,
Whether meal or snack so small.

Good things to eat.
Good things to eat.
Good things to eat.
God gives them all to me.

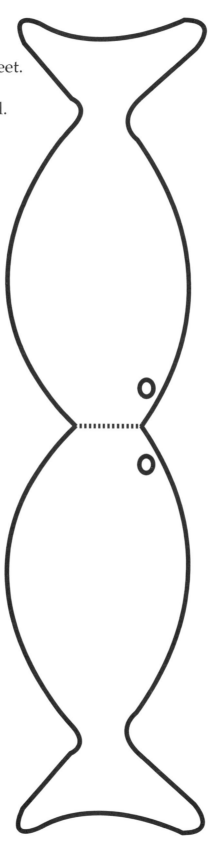

## snack/song

### What You Need
- duplicated page
- tape
- scissors
- bread
- mandarin oranges, drained
- peanut butter
- almond slices
- candy-coated pieces

### What to Do
1. Have the children cut out the fish and tape it together at one end.
2. Encourage the students to write a prayer on the fish.
3. To prepare the snack, tear the crust off the bread and tear the bread in half.
4. Spread peanut butter on the bread.
5. Place two orange slices, outside edges together, on the end of the bread for the tail.
6. Stick almonds in the peanut butter for scales.
7. Place a candy in the peanut butter for an eye.
8. Sing the song to the tune of "Jesus Loves Me" before you eat.

**ANDREW**

# Memory Verse Puzzle

## game

### What You Need
- star pattern
- yellow poster board
- crayons

### What to Do
1. Duplicate several copies of the star on yellow poster board and cut them out.
2. Have the students form partners.
3. Give each team a puzzle and see who can get the star put together the fastest.
4. The first one finished should say, "I'm gonna shine!"

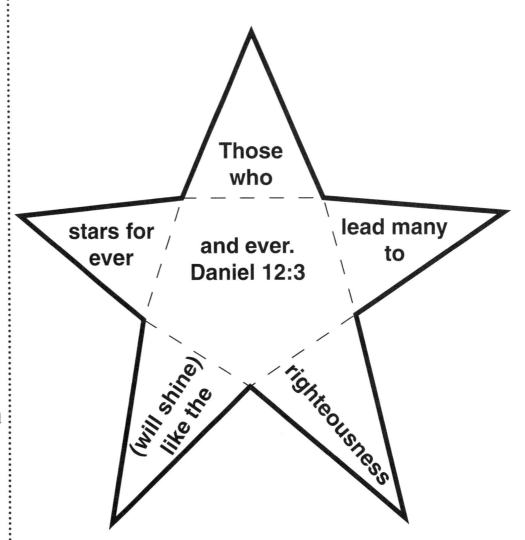

Those who

stars for ever

and ever.
Daniel 12:3

lead many to

(will shine) like the

righteousness

ANDREW

14

# Shine Like the Stars

I'll shine like the stars forever.
I'll shine like the stars forever.
I'll shine like the stars forever.
If I bring others to Christ.

Daniel twelve, verse three,
Daniel twelve, verse three.
Daniel twelve, verse three,
Says like stars, we shall be.

## craft/song

### What You Need
- duplicated page
- glue
- glitter
- paint brush
- tape
- scissors

### What to Do
1. Have the students cut out the star with handle.
2. Instruct the children to paint glue on the star and sprinkle it with glitter. Allow to dry.
3. Show how to fold the handle on the dashed lines and tape the ends to the back of the star.
4. Sing the song to the tune of "For He's A Jolly Good Fellow" while "twinkling" the stars.

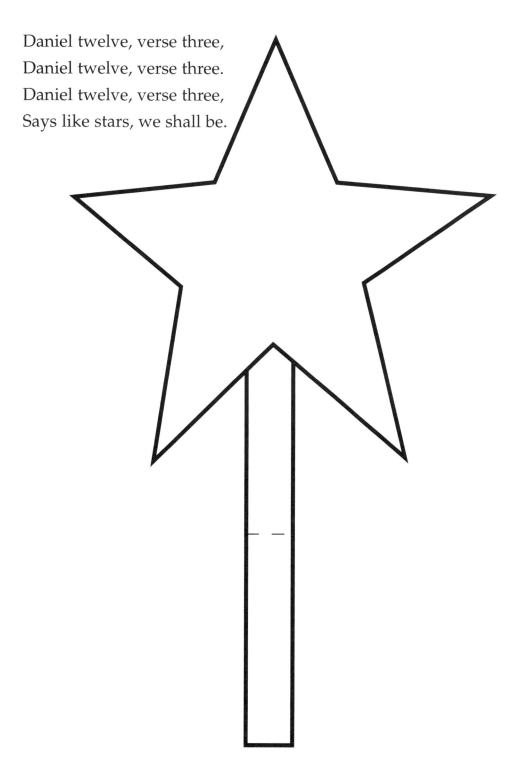

**ANDREW**

## craft

### What You Need
- duplicated page
- yellow paper
- markers

### What to Do
1. Show how to fold yellow paper, accordion-style, to make three sections.
2. Give each child a star pattern and show how to trace it on the top section and cut it out through all the layers, being careful not to cut on the fold.
3. Have the students unfold the stars and write, "If I lead many to Jesus I will shine like the stars for ever and ever."
4. Encourage the students to tape the stars to their mirror at home to remind them to tell others about Jesus.

**ANDREW**

# Star Room Reminder

# Chapter 2
# James, Full of Zeal

## Memory Verse

*It is fine to be zealous, provided the purpose is good.* Galatians 4:18

## Story to Share
## Eyewitness to a Miracle

Jairus was the head of the synagogue, the Jewish place of worship. He was an important man, but all his importance couldn't help him. His daughter was dying.

Jairus ran to Jesus. "Jesus, please help me. My little girl is dying. Will You come and put Your hands on her and make her well?"

Jesus loved children. Nodding to Jairus, He started through the crowd. Before they reached the house, they heard the pipers playing music and people wailing. "Oh no," sobbed the man. "We're too late. She is already dead."

As they reached the house, the wailing stopped. "Why are You here?" they asked Jesus. "You can't do anything. She is already dead."

James was with Jesus. He listened to hear what Jesus would say.

"She's not dead," said Jesus. "She's just sleeping."

James frowned as he heard the sounds of disbelief coming from the mourners. Some openly laughed.

"Come," said Jesus to James, Peter and John as He went into the house with Jairus.

James looked at the small girl. She did look dead, but he knew if Jesus said she was sleeping, then she was sleeping. He watched as Jesus gently took her tiny hand and said, "Little daughter, it's time to get up."

James knew he was seeing another miracle as the little girl sat up in bed. She rubbed her eyes and then stood up. "Mother and Father," she said as she hugged both her parents, "I'm hungry."

James laughed as he watched the joy on the parents' faces. Jesus smiled, too. "Give your daughter something to eat," He said.

James couldn't help but touch Jesus' hand, the hand that had healed many. Jesus smiled as James said, "Blessed be the name of Jesus."

— Luke 8:41-42, 49-56

## Discussion Questions

1. What did Jairus ask of Jesus? (to heal his daughter)
2. Did Jesus get to the home too late? (no, but she was dead)
3. What was James' response to Jesus' healing? (praise)

## puzzle

### What You Need
- duplicated page
- pencils
- Bibles

### What to Do
1. Give each child a duplicated page, a pencil and a Bible.
2. Read the instructions aloud.
3. If students have difficulty, allow them to look up the Scripture in a Bible. The answer is on page 93.

### What to Say
What do you get excited about? Is there an activity you love so much you talk to everyone you meet about it? When we say James was "full of zeal," we mean he was excited about his love for Jesus and His work. Our memory verse says it is good to be full of zeal if what you are zealous about is good.

**JAMES**

# Full of Zeal

Oops, the verse got zealous about Zs. Can you substitute them for vowels — except for the one that is needed?

Zt zs fznz tz bz
zzzlzzs, przvzdzd
thz pzrpzsz
zs gzzd.
Gzlztzzns 4:18

_____

_____

_____

_____

_____

# Get Up and Walk

## game

### What You Need
• hand pattern

### What to Do
1. Before class, cut out the hand.
2. Instruct the students to sit in a circle. Choose one to be James and give the hand to him or her.
3. James should walk around the circle, then choose someone to be the sick girl by placing the hand on his or her head and saying, "Get up."
4. The chosen one should grab the hand, jump up and chase James around the circle and back to the empty spot. The object is for James to be seated in the circle before being tagged with the hand.

**JAMES**

# It's Time to Get Up

**What You Need**
- duplicated page
- crayons
- scissors
- glue

**What to Do**

1. Give each student a duplicated page and instruct the students to color and cut out the bed and daughter.
2. Show how to glue the daughter to the bed, gluing only below the dashed line.
3. Demonstrate how the daughter can obey Jesus' words, "My daughter, it's time to get up" by sitting her up in bed.

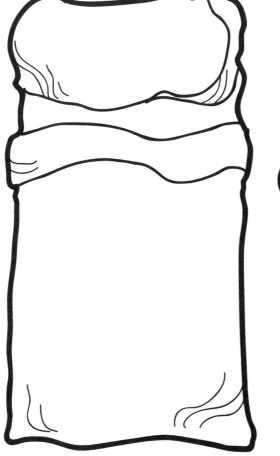

**JAMES**

# Obedience Is Important

James saw the little girl,
Little girl, little girl.
James saw the little girl.
Sick, sick girl.

Jesus said, "Please sit up,
Please sit up, please sit up."
Jesus said, "Please sit up,
Sick, sick girl."

James saw the girl obey,
Girl obey, girl obey.
James saw the girl obey.
She is well.

**What You Need**
• duplicated page

**What to Do**
1. Ask, **What would have happened if Jairus' daughter didn't obey Jesus when He said to get up? She had learned to obey her parents so it was easy to obey God. Do you obey your parents?**
2. Give each child a copy of the song. Sing it to the tune of "London Bridge."

**JAMES**

# Sons of Thunder

## craft

### What You Need
• duplicated page
• thread
• hole punch
• crayons
• scissors
• tape

### What to Do
1. Have the students color the clouds and lightning.
2. Show how to punch holes where indicated and tie a length of thread through the holes.
3. Let the students help you attach the clouds to the ceiling with tape for a room decoration.

### What to Say
Jesus nicknamed James and his brother, John, "Sons of Thunder." What are some characteristics of thunder? (loud, deafening, crashing) Why do you think Jesus called the two men by that name? (that's how they acted in their service to God)

**JAMES**

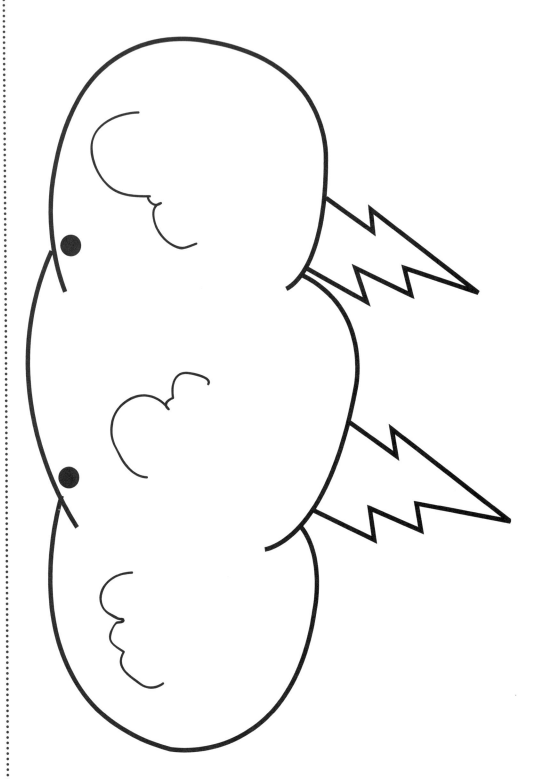

# Zealous Students

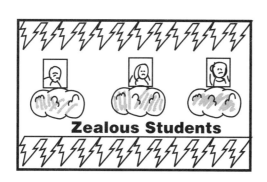

Zealous Students

## bulletin board

### What You Need
- cloud and lightning patterns, pp. 25-26
- white poster paper
- yellow paper
- dark chalk
- stencils
- black marker
- facial tissue
- instant camera

### What to Do
1. Cover the board with white paper.
2. Trace or copy the lightning on yellow paper. Cut it out and attach it around the board for a border.
3. Stencil or cut out the title and attach it to the board.
4. Write the memory verse on the board.
5. Allow the students to color a cloud with dark chalk and rub it with a tissue.
6. Bring a camera to class and snap a picture of each student. They should punch a fist in the air to show how zealous they are about God's work.
7. Attach the clouds at the bottom of the students' pictures and arrange them on the board.

**JAMES**

# Chapter 3
# John, Disciple of Love

## Memory Verse

*Let us not love with words or tongue but with actions and in truth.* 1 John 3:18

## Story to Share
## A Special Assignment

Jesus loved John. He loved all His disciples, but John was especially dear to Him. John was probably the youngest of Jesus' disciples and may have seemed like a younger brother to Jesus.

Wherever Jesus was, John made sure he was closest to Him. His love for Jesus overflowed from his heart.

One day, the disciples were eating together. "Friends," said Jesus, "one of you here is going to betray Me."

John was the closest to Jesus and Peter motioned to him. "John, ask Jesus what He means."

John leaned back until his head was resting on Jesus' chest. "Jesus, we don't understand. What do You mean?"

Jesus took some bread and dipped it into the bowl in front of Him. "Whomever I give this bread to is the one who will betray Me." Then Jesus handed the bread to Judas.

The day came when, because of the betrayal, Jesus was crucified. John was there, again close to Jesus even as He was dying. Jesus' mother, Mary, was also there, crying as she saw the agony Jesus was feeling.

Jesus looked down from the cross. "John, please take care of My mother," He said.

Jesus didn't need to ask John more than once. When Jesus died, John led Mary away from the cross.

"Come, Mother Mary. You will live with me," he said. From that day on, wherever John lived, he made a place for Jesus' mother.

— based on John 19:17-27

## Discussion Questions

1. Jesus had a special assignment for John. What was it? (to care for His mother)
2. Why did John do what Jesus asked of him? (he loved Jesus)

## craft

### What You Need
- duplicated page
- yarn
- scissors
- glue
- hole punch

### What to Do
1. Have the students color and cut out the hand and arm.
2. Show how to glue the hand on the back of the arm.
3. Instruct the students to fill out the chore promise.
4. Show how to punch holes where indicated.
5. Help the students thread yarn through the holes and tie the ends together in a bow.
6. Encourage the students to hang the arm on a family member's bedroom door to pledge their love.

### What to Say
What can you do for someone this week to show your love? It shouldn't be a chore you already do, but a chore that belongs to a family member.

**JOHN**

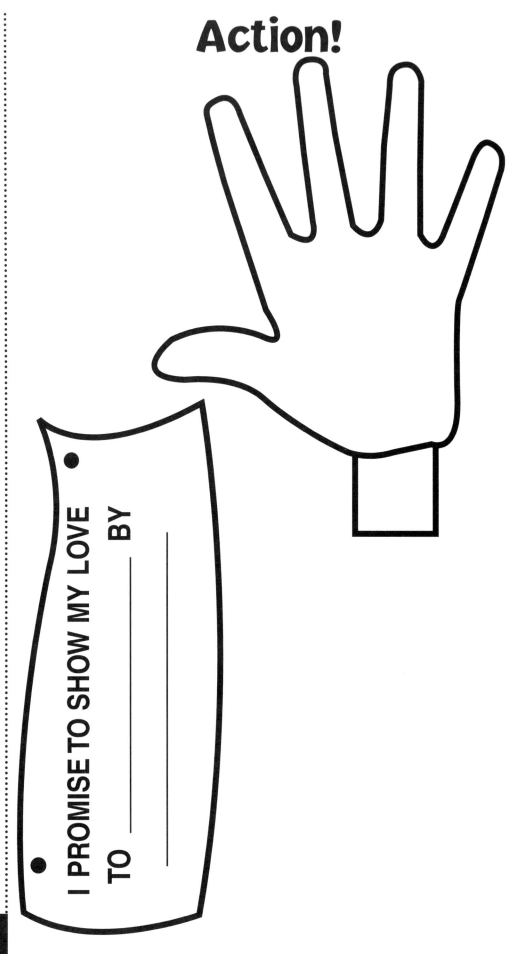

## Action!

I PROMISE TO SHOW MY LOVE

TO _____

BY _____

28

# The Greatest Love

## craft

### What You Need
- heart pattern
- red poster board
- 1 t. creamy toothpaste
- 2 t. white glue
- 4 t. cornstarch
- brown tempera paint (or water)

### What to Do
1. Duplicate the heart on red poster board for each child.
2. Have the students cut out a heart.
3. Mix the toothpaste, glue and cornstarch. Gradually add water and mix until it cleans the side of the bowl. Knead until smooth.
4. Show how to form a cross from the dough (it will dry fast).
5. Have the students carefully glue the cross onto the heart. The cross will dry completely in 18 hours.

### What To Say

Jesus showed by His actions that He loved people. How did He show Jairus He loved him? (by healing his daughter) How did Jesus show the 5,000 people who had come to hear Him teach that He loved them? (He fed them) Can you think of other ways Jesus loved with actions? What was the greatest way of all He showed His love? (by dying on the cross)

**JOHN**

29

# Heart-y Snack

## snack/craft

### What You Need

- 5 c. sweetened alphabet-shaped cereal
- 1 c. red cinnamon hearts
- 2 c. printed candy hearts
- 1 c. raisins
- 1 c. pretzel sticks, broken in half
- duplicated page
- red ink pad
- disposable hand wipes
- plastic sandwich bags
- napkins
- scissors
- hole punch

### What to Do

1. Before class, combine the cereal, candy and raisins in a large container. Put the lid on it and shake it to mix. Pour some into sandwich bags for the students and keep the remainder for an in-class snack.
2. Give each child a duplicated page. Have them cut out the tag and fold it on the dashed line so that the words are inside.
3. Show how to press a finger onto the stamp pad and
   *continued at right*

## JOHN

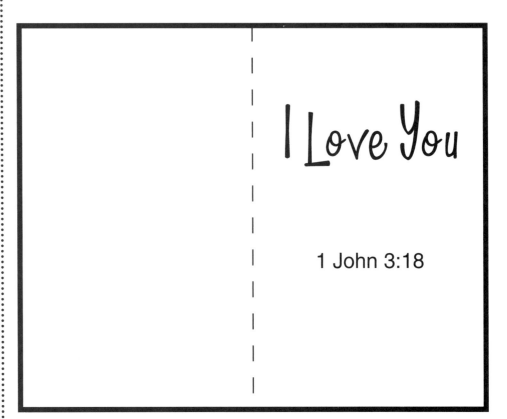

I Love You

1 John 3:18

### What to Do, *continued*

place it in the middle of the front cover of the tag, angling left. Then press it again and place it on the tag angling right and forming a heart. Clean hands with disposable wipes.

4. Help the students punch a hole in the corner of the card and tie a ribbon in it.
5. Give each child a sandwich bag with snack mix in it.
6. Show how to tie the ribbon and tag onto the bag.
7. Give each child a half-cup of snack mix on a napkin to enjoy.

# Helpful Charades

**What You Need**
• duplicated pp. 31-32
• basket

**What to Do**
1. Cut out and fold the cards. Place them in a basket.
2. Divide the class into two teams.
3. To play, have one person from the first team pick a charade. That player has 1 or 2 minutes to stand up and communicate the love charade without saying a word. If the team guesses it, they get to keep the points for that charade. If not, the other team has a chance to guess the charade.
4. Continue taking turns until the charades have all been acted out. The team with the most points wins.

**JOHN**

# Kids to Love

### What You Need
• duplicated page
• pencils

### What to Do

1. Give each student a frame and instruct the students to draw a hat at the top of it, then fold the paper in fourths.

2. The students should hand the paper to the person on their right. Each one then draws a head and neck on the paper and folds it closed.

3. The students again hand the paper to the one on the right and draw a body in and fold it back.

4. Again, the students hand the paper to the one on the right, drawing the legs and feet.

5. One at a time, have the students open the papers. Allow each one to choose a "friend" (drawing). (This is a fun activity when the wiggles seem to get the best of your class. It will release the giggles and the students will be ready to quiet down.)

**JOHN**

# LOVEly Verse

## game

### What You Need
- blindfold
- verse token

### What to Do
1. Form a circle with chairs. Have all of the students except one sit in a chair.
2. Blindfold the one chosen to be It. It should walk around the inside of the circle, then sit on someone's lap, saying, "What's the verse?"
3. Whomever's lap It is sitting on says the verse in a fake voice.
4. If It can identify the speaker, the speaker becomes It.
5. Allow the students to use the tokens until they become familiar with the verse.

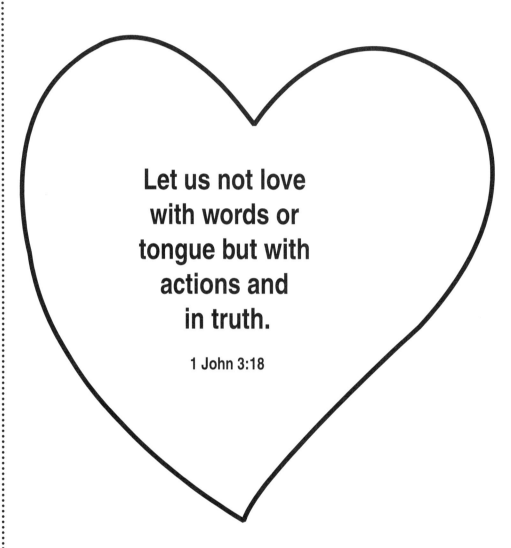

Let us not love with words or tongue but with actions and in truth.

1 John 3:18

**JOHN**

# Show Your Love

Do more than say the words.
Do more than say the words.
Show your love with actions.
And "I love you" will be heard.

## song/game

### What You Need
• heart pattern
• colored paper
• scissors

### What to Do
1. Duplicate the heart pattern on colored paper. Cut out several copies.
2. Place the hearts on the floor, one less than the number of students.
3. Sing the song to the tune of "The Farmer in the Dell," stopping anywhere in the song.
4. When the song stops, the students must sit down on a heart or they are out.
5. Remove one heart before each round. Whoever sits on the last heart wins!

**JOHN**

35

### What You Need
- duplicated page
- Bibles
- pencils

### What to Do
1. Give each child a duplicated page, a Bible and a pencil.
2. Have the students look up the Scripture and fill in the blanks. The answers are on page 93.
3. This may also be used as a class activity. The one who finds the verse first can stand, read the verse and choose someone to tell who showed love.

# Who Showed Love?

Read the scriptures to find who showed love.

## Genesis 14:14-15

A _____

## 1 Samuel 20:17

D _____ and J _____

## 2 Kings 4:32-34

E _____

## Matthew 2:11

W _____

## Luke 5:13

J _____

## John 12:3

M _____

## Luke 10:33-34

S _____

## John 3:16

G _____

# Chapter 4
# Peter, a Natural Leader

## 📖 Memory Verse

*Simon Peter answered, "You are the Christ, the Son of the living God."* Matthew 16:16

## Story to Share
## Peter Leads the Meeting

It had been 50 days since Jesus had risen from the dead. Jesus had returned to heaven to live with His Father, God. Before Jesus left, He said, "Don't leave Jerusalem until you have received the gift of the Holy Spirit."

The disciples waited for this gift. Now it was the day of the Jewish harvest festival, Pentecost. The disciples were gathered in one room. "Peter, when do you think the Holy Spirit Jesus told us about will come?" asked Thomas.

"The Holy Spirit will come when it is time," answered Peter. "Jesus said we would receive this helper and His word is true."

Just then the disciples heard a sound like a mighty wind rushing through the house where they were. They looked at each other, startled at this loud noise. Then they saw flames flickering over the head of each disciple. Joy flooded their hearts as they realized the gift of the Holy Spirit had come.

Because of the Pentecost festival, there were Jews from every nation visiting Jerusalem. The strange sound of wind drew a crowd.

"Did you hear that noise?"

"Yes, it sounded like wind blowing."

The disciples began talking to the crowd about Jesus. The disciples were speaking their own Galilean language but everyone of all other languages could understand what they were saying!

"What is this?" asked one. "How can we all understand them?"

"They must have had too much to drink," answered another.

Peter heard what the men were saying. Holding his hands in front of him to quiet the crowd he said, "No, these men are not drunk. These men have the Holy Spirit to guide them."

The crowd grew quiet as Peter started to preach to them.

He told them of the miracles Jesus performed, and how He had died on the cross and then rose from the grave. He told them how Jesus had gone back to heaven and one day would come back for those who were saved.

"How can we become saved?" the crowd began asking.

"Repent of your sins," urged Peter. "Turn away from your sin and be baptized."

Because Peter explained salvation, about 3,000 people became Christians that day.

— based on Acts, chapter 2

## ❓ Discussion Questions

1. Who in our story had the gift of leadership? (Peter)
2. If you do not have this gift, what can you do to help? (Be an excellent follower; use other gifts)
3. Why did Peter follow Jesus? (Peter believed in Him.)

**puzzle**

**What You Need**
• duplicated page
• pencils

**What to Do**
1. Give each child a duplicated page and a pencil.
2. Read the instructions aloud. Help those who have difficulty.
3. The answers are on page 93.

# Following Peter's Example

Peter was born in a Jewish home. As a boy he would have gone to a synagogue school where he learned portions of the Law and the Prophets. Years later, when he was a disciple of Jesus, he was still able to quote Scripture from memory.

Can you help Peter get this verse back in order?

| 1+1 answered | 2+2 Christ | 3+3 Simon | 4+4 living | 5+5 Son | 6+6 Peter |
|---|---|---|---|---|---|

| 7+7 the | 8+8 of | 9+9 You | 10+10 the | 11+11 God | 12+12 are |
|---|---|---|---|---|---|

| 13+13 Matthew 16:16 | 14+14 the |
|---|---|

_____    _____    _____,  "_____    _____
6                12              2                18              24

_____    _____    _____    _____    _____
20              4                28              10              16

_____    _____    _____."  _____
14              8                22              26

**PETER**

# Come!

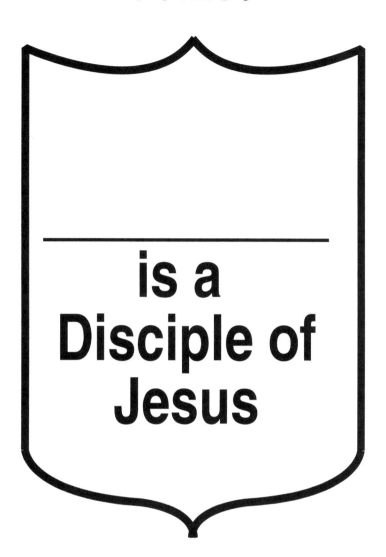

_____ is a Disciple of Jesus

## craft/song

**What You Need**
- duplicated page
- glue
- scissors
- craft pin

**What to Do**
1. Have the students color and cut out the badge. They should write their name on the line.
2. Help the children glue the badge to a craft pin.
3. After the glue has dried, assist the students in putting on the badge.
4. Teach the song to the tune of "Stop and Let Me Tell You" and do the motions.

Come, be My disciple.          ("come" motion)

Peter heard the Savior say.     (cup ear)

Come, be My disciple.

Peter heard the Savior say.

Peter, leave your boats and
come follow Me.              (rowing motion)

I'll show you how to be saved, you will see.

Come, be My disciple.

Peter heard the Savior say.

**PETER**

## game

### What You Need

- duplicated page
- paper grocery sacks
- scissors
- stapler or glue
- dry beans
- markers
- bucket

### What to Do

1. Trace the fish pattern on the grocery sacks. You will need two fish for each child.
2. Have the students write their name on one fish.
3. Place a pile of beans on the middle of the fish. Place another fish on top and glue or staple the two together.
4. Have the children form a line. Place a bucket two feet from the starting line. Each child should throw his or her fish over a shoulder, trying to throw it in the bucket. Award 3 points for each fish in the bucket and 1 point for each fish that touches the bucket.

**PETER**

# I'll Follow You

### What To Say

When Jesus wanted Peter to be His disciple, Peter had a decision to make: "Should I follow Jesus or continue fishing?" What decision did he make? Are you willing to give up your plans for Jesus?

# Freaky Fish

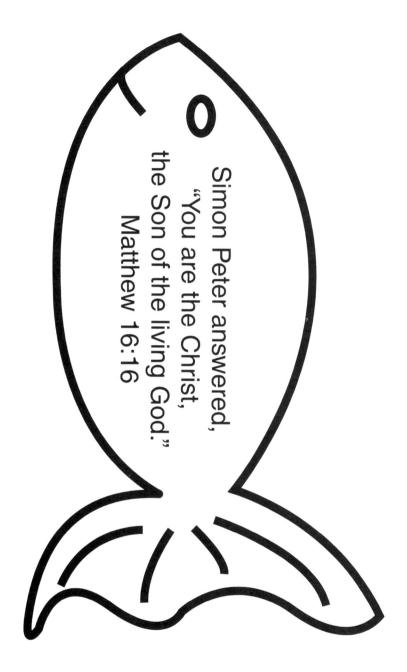

Simon Peter answered,
"You are the Christ,
the Son of the living God."
Matthew 16:16

## snack

### What You Need

- tortillas
- raisins
- cheese
- pretzels
- spray cheese
- popcorn
- olives
- pickles
- bowls
- paper plates
- duplicated page

### What to Do

1. Provide the ingredients above or any combination of food you desire.
2. Say, **Using these ingredients, what kind of fish can you come up with? Just remember — you have to eat your creation!**
3. Allow the children to arrange the food items in a fish shape on a paper plate.
4. Have the students vote on the best fish, the prettiest fish and the ugliest fish.
5. Allow the children to cut out a Freaky Fish bookmark to place in their Bible as a reminder that they should be disciples of Jesus.

**PETER**

## puzzle

### What You Need
• duplicated page
• pencils

### What to Do
1. Give each child a duplicated page and a pencil.
2. Read the instructions aloud. Assist students who have difficulty.
3. The answers are on page 93.

# Peter's Name

Peter's original name was Simon. But Jesus gave him a new name: Cephas (or Peter). What does the name "Peter" mean? Unscramble the words below and place the circled letters on the line below that.

Peter was a __ __ __ __ __ ⃝ __ __ __          IHREMFSNA
                                                (Luke 5:2)

Peter's first name was __ __ __ ⃝ __          NISMO
                                                (John 1:40)

Jesus called Peter ⃝ __ __ __ __ __          PSHACE
                                                (John 1:42)

Peter once saw Jesus __ __ __ ⃝ on the water          KAWL
                                                (John 6:19)

Peter's name means "the ____ ____ ____ ____."
Jesus gave Simon the name "Peter" because Jesus knew
Peter would be the earthly leader of the new church after
Jesus returned to be with God in heaven. (Matthew 16:17-19)

**PETER**

42

# Peter's Impressions

## craft

### What You Need
- duplicated page
- bright crayons
- medium grade sandpaper
- newspapers
- iron
- white construction paper

### What to Do
1. Have the students trace the water and boat on sandpaper.
2. Instruct the children to color the picture, pressing hard. They may add a sun, birds or a sunset. The students can write Peter's name in the waves, but remind them to write it backwards because this is a transfer.
3. Lay newspapers on the table. Show how to place the sandpaper on the newspaper, picture side up. Place a sheet of construction paper over the sandpaper.
4. Iron over the top of the construction paper (iron should be on low) until the crayon melts. Remove the paper. Allow to cool. **Note:** Do not leave the iron unattended.

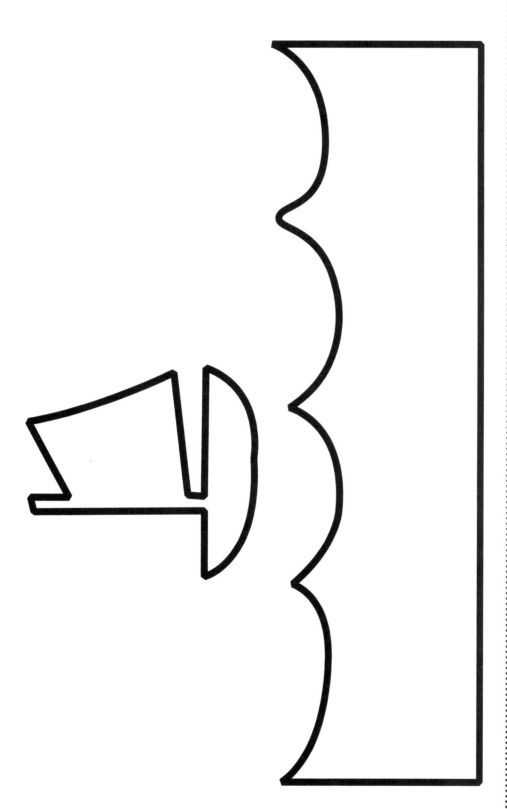

**PETER**

# Tongues of Fire

## craft

### What You Need
- duplicated page
- unopened soup can
- cardboard
- glue
- stamp pad
- crayons
- scissors

### What to Do
1. Instruct the students to cut out the frame and the flame.
2. Have the students color inside the letters of "Holy Spirit."
3. Show how to trace several tongues of fire onto cardboard and cut them out. Allow the students to glue several flames to a can.
4. Show how to roll the soup can on an ink pad, then roll the can on the plaque to decorate the frame. (Students may want to try the roller on other paper before using it on their plaques.)

# Precious Peter

Peter wrote two books of the Bible: 1 Peter and 2 Peter. Peter liked to use the word "precious" in his writing. Look up the verses below and find out what was precious to Peter.

2 Peter 1:1     Precious     F_____

1 Peter 1:19    Precious     B_____

1 Peter 2:6     Precious     C_____

2 Peter 1:4     Precious     P_____

What is precious to you? Draw a picture below of something you value.

## puzzle

· · · · · · · · · · · ·

### What You Need
• duplicated page
• pencils

### What to Do
1. Give each child a duplicated page and a pencil.
2. Read the instructions aloud. Assist students who have difficulty.
3. The answers are on page 93.

**PETER**

# Chapter 5
# Matthew, the Disciple Who Left It All

## 📖 Memory Verse

*Everyone who has left houses or brothers or sisters or father or mother or children or fields for my sake...will inherit eternal life.* Matthew 19:29

## Story to Share
## A Greater Miracle

Jesus was in the region of the Gadarenes when He saw two demon-possessed men. The men were so violent that they scared anyone who saw them. Jesus spoke, and the demons left the men and entered into a herd of pigs. The demons so overtook the pigs that they rushed into the water and drowned.

The men who owned the pigs were angry. "Now we don't have any pigs," they said. "Why did you do that? Leave and don't come back."

Jesus did as He was asked. He left and went to Capernaum. When the people saw that Jesus was there they began bringing the sick, lame and blind to Him for healing.

One man was too sick to reach Jesus. Instead, his friends brought him on a mat. Jesus saw the faith of the friends and healed the man.

"What a miracle," those around Him said.

Matthew, a tax collector, was sitting at his tax booth attending to his business. "Did you hear about the miracle today?" someone asked him.

"No, what happened?"

"Jesus healed a man who was too sick to walk."

"Look!" said another. "Here He comes now."

Matthew raised his head to search for this man of miracles. When he did, his eyes met those of Jesus.

"Come and follow Me," said Jesus quietly.

Without hesitation, Matthew rose and left his job. He would follow Jesus, the Son of God. When Matthew felt the peace which came with following Jesus, he said, "This miracle of my heart is greater than the healing of a man or the casting out of demons. This miracle is the greatest of all."

## ❓ Discussion Questions

1. What was Matthew's occupation before he followed Jesus? (a tax collector)
2. Did Matthew make more money following Jesus? (no)
3. Why did Matthew follow Jesus? (Matthew believed in Him.)

# 1, 2, 3

1 little, 2 little, 3 little pennies.
4 little, 5 little, 6 little pennies.
7 little, 8 little, 9 little pennies.
10 pennies counted Matthew.

1 little, 2 little, 3 little people,
4 little, 5 little, 6 little people,
7 little, 8 little, 9 little people,
10 people loved by Matthew.

## craft/song

### What You Need
- duplicated page
- crayons
- tape
- scissors

### What to Do
1. Have the students color and cut out the finger puppet.
2. Show how to tape the ends together and fit the puppet over your fingers.
3. Sing the song together to the tune of "Ten Little Indians."

### What to Say
Matthew loved money until he met Jesus. From that day, he wanted to tell others about Jesus. First he counted money, then he counted people!

**MATTHEW**

## puzzle

### What You Need
• duplicated page
• pencils

### What to Do
1. Give each child a duplicated page and a pencil.
2. Read the instructions aloud. This would also be a good time to discuss putting Jesus first. Say, **This scripture doesn't mean for you to pack your bags and leave home. Jesus is saying that we should love Him best and put Him first.**
3. The answer key is on page 94.

# Hidden Verse

Find the underlined words of the memory verse in the puzzle below it.

EVERYONE WHO HAS <u>LEFT</u> <u>HOUSES</u> OR <u>BROTHERS</u> OR <u>SISTERS</u> OR <u>FATHER</u> OR <u>MOTHER</u> OR <u>CHILDREN</u> OR <u>FIELDS</u> FOR MY SAKE…WILL <u>INHERIT</u> <u>ETERNAL</u> <u>LIFE</u>.

MATTHEW 19:29

```
F R F G V F F K B N R G P Z
R O O P L R H I G W D E U S L
E T N W V O B Q O S S H V R F
F K T G U M G T A R F T D E U
I V E S P T F K E Z U A T T B
L H E T I R E H N I I F S S H
H S Z C L T T M O I T C D I M
R X U E E O F A Y S T H L S O
T U F R R G D U N S W I E N T
U T N B V Z X L P X X L I P H
D A N E N O Y R E V E D F U E
L Z Y O J H I L P D F R W J R
X X E T D J Q Z X U D E M V D
A F U F H F K T Z N K N Y U E
S R E H T A F X M Y W H U T M
```

**MATTHEW**

48

# Leaving It All

Color the squares below that answer the questions. The remaining two squares will be the answer to the question at the bottom.

1. Two yummy foods
2. Three colors
3. Three words which begin with the letter B
4. Two names which begin with the letter M

| | | | |
|---|---|---|---|
| Matthew | Blue | Pizza | Eternal |
| Bible | Red | Life | Baby |
| Cake | Mary | Ball | Pink |

When we put Jesus first, we will inherit

_____  _____.

## puzzle

### What You Need
- duplicated page
- crayons
- pencils

### What to Do
1. Give each child a duplicated page and some crayons.
2. Read the instructions aloud.
3. The answer is on page 93.

**MATTHEW**

# Matthew's Ink

## craft

### What You Need
- duplicated page
- 1 c. powdered milk
- ¾ c. water
- blue food coloring
- wooden skewers
- plastic nut cups or film cases
- scissors

### What to Do
1. Have the children help you mix the milk, water and food coloring together.
2. Pour the ink into individual containers for each student.
3. Show how to use a skewer to dip in the "ink" and write JESUS on the plaque.
4. Allow the students to cut out the plaque to hang in their rooms.

# Pig Pong

### game

- - - - - - - - - - -

## What You Need

- pig pattern
- pink paper
- paint stirrers
- ping pong balls
- scissors
- glue
- poster board

## What to Do

1. Cut out the pig and trace around it twice on poster board. Cut out the poster board pig.
2. Glue a paint stirrer to the back of each pig. Glue extra poster board on top of both stirrers for stability.
3. The students should bat the ball back and forth with the paddles, saying a word of the memory verse as they hit the ball. The first time one misses he gets a P, the next time I, the next a G. The first one to spell PIG is out and a new player is chosen.
4. This game also provides a good way to review the disciples. For a change of pace in the game, have the players call out the name of a disciple as they hit the ball.

**MATTHEW**

## What To Say

The men who were angry about their lost pigs had a big problem — they were selfish! They cared more about their pigs than other people. What is more important to you? Your toys or your friends?

## craft/game

### What You Need

- rice cake
- peanut butter
- raisins
- large marshmallows
- shoestring licorice
- duplicated page
- scissors
- plastic knives
- basket

### What to Do

1. Have the students spread peanut butter on a rice cake.
2. Show how to flatten a marshmallow and poke two raisins in the top. Place the marshmallow on the bottom half of the rice cake. This is the pig's body and feet.
3. Instruct the students to press two raisins in the rice cake for eyes.
4. Help the children cut a licorice string in half. Show how to curl it around a finger and poke it in the side of the rice cake for a tail.
5. Instruct the students to write their name on the duplicated tail and cut it out.

## MATTHEW

# Piggy Snacks
## Questions

1. Who wrote the first book in the New Testament? (Matthew)
2. Quote the memory verse.
3. What was wrong with the two men Jesus saw? (They were demon-possessed.)
4. Quote the memory verse.
5. Jesus spoke to the demons, instructing them to leave the men. Where did they go? (into the pigs)
6. Quote the memory verse.
7. Were the pig owners happy with Jesus? (no)
8. Quote the memory verse.
9. How did the sick man's friends bring him to Jesus? (on a mat)
10. Quote the memory verse.
11. Who heard about Jesus healing this man? (Matthew)
12. Quote the memory verse.
13. What was Matthew's occupation before he met Jesus? (tax collector)
14. Quote the memory verse.
15. What was the greatest miracle of all according to Matthew? (miracle in his heart)

tail

### What to Do, *continued*

6. Put all of the tails in a basket.
7. One by one, pull out a tail. Ask a question and call out the **name** of the person on the tail. That person will stand, **oink** and say the answer. All the other pigs will oink if it is the correct answer and grunt if it is incorrect. The students may answer the question wrong on purpose to try and trick the other pigs.

# Tax Collector Matthew

Look up the scriptures.  Write the types of money on the line that are given in the Scripture.

Matthew 18:24  _____

Matthew 10:9  _____

Now read what it says about money in 1 Timothy 6:10 and write it on the line below.

_____

_____

_____

Does it say that having money is a sin?

What is sin? ___ ___ ___ ___ of money.

## What You Need
• duplicated page
• Bibles
• pencils

## What to Do
1. Give each child a duplicated page, a Bible and a pencil.
2. Read the instructions. Assist children who have difficulty.
3. The answers are on page 93.

## What to Say
Before Matthew became a disciple of Jesus, he was a tax collector.  Because Matthew knew a lot about money, when he wrote his gospel he used stories from the job he left.

**MATTHEW**

# The Sick Man's Mat

## What You Need
- duplicated page
- glue
- scissors
- colored pencils

## What to Do
1. Give each child two copies of strips.
2. Allow the children to color the mat strips and cut them out.
3. Instruct the students to place five strips down on the table.
4. Show how to lay a strip on top of the first strip, under the next and so on, weaving it through all five. Continue until the mat is woven.
5. Help the children carefully glue the ends in place. Have them write their names on their mats. Use at snack time!

**MATTHEW**

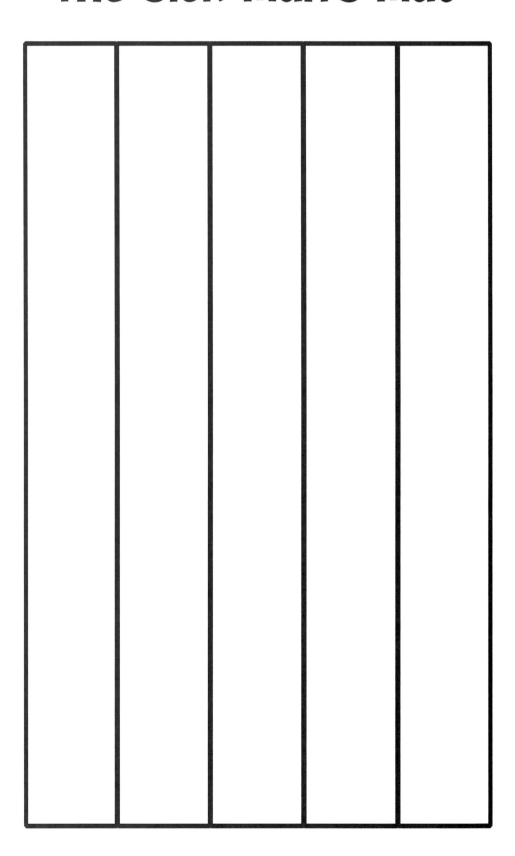

54

# Chapter 6
# Judas, Lover of Money

## 📖 Memory Verse

*Some people, eager for money, have wandered from the faith.* 1 Timothy 6:10

## 📖 Story to Share
## All for 30 Silver Pieces

Judas loved money. He was the treasurer for the disciples. He loved to bargain and was good with figures. But, there were times when Judas took money from the treasury to make his own personal finances grow.

When Mary anointed Jesus with the costly ointment, Judas was the first to complain. "That ointment is worth a lot of money," he said, "almost what a man would make in working a year. I can't believe she just threw it way. It should have been sold to feed the poor."

Later, some men came to Judas. "Judas, we want to arrest Jesus and need your help."

"What will you give me?" asked Judas.

"Thirty pieces of silver. Just show us which man is Jesus so we can arrest Him."

Thirty pieces of silver was the price of a slave when killed by a beast. Surely the Son of God was worth more than that! But Judas' love of money made it easy for him to make up his mind. He loved money more than he loved Jesus. "I'll do it," he said.

Jesus and His disciples had been praying in the Garden of Gethsemane when Judas led the large group to where He was. The men were all armed with swords and clubs. The burning torches they carried lit up the dark night.

Judas went up to Jesus and gave Him a kiss. That was the signal for the men to arrest Jesus. "Teacher," he said.

Jesus looked at Judas with tears in His eyes. "Judas, you have betrayed the Son of God with a kiss."

Judas knew he had done a horrible thing. Jesus had loved him and taught him. Judas had watched him perform miracles. The One he had betrayed was God's Son. Without another word, Judas turned away as the men grabbed Jesus.

What pain was in Judas' heart! He traded 30 pieces of silver for betraying a sinless man. Too late, Judas realized there was no price that would be great enough to exchange for Jesus.

— based on Matthew 26:47-50, 27:1-4

## ❓❓ Discussion Questions

1. Is there any money that would equal the cost of Jesus? (no)

2. Is there anything more important to you than Jesus?

# C-R-O-S-S

## game

### What You Need
- duplicated page
- paper sack
- scissors
- glue

### What to Do
1. Make three copies of the letters. Cut out the letters and place them in a paper sack.
2. Cut out a cross and glue it on the front of the sack.
3. Divide the class into teams. Ask the questions. For a correct answer, a teammate may choose a letter out of the bag. If it is a letter the team needs to spell CROSS, the player may keep the letter. If not, the letter goes back into the bag. The first team to spell CROSS wins.

## Questions

1. What did Judas love more than Jesus? (money)
2. Quote the memory verse.
3. Who was the treasurer for the disciples? (Judas)
4. How did Judas' own personal finances grow? (He took money from the disciples' treasury.)
5. Quote the memory verse.
6. Who anointed Jesus with costly ointment? (Mary)
7. What did the evil men offer Judas to show them which man was Jesus? (30 pieces of silver)
8. Quote the memory verse.
9. Where was Jesus praying when Judas led the men to Him? (Garden of Gethsemane)
10. How did Judas show who Jesus was? (He kissed Him.)
11. Quote the memory verse.
12. Was Judas happy with the money he received for selling Jesus? (no)

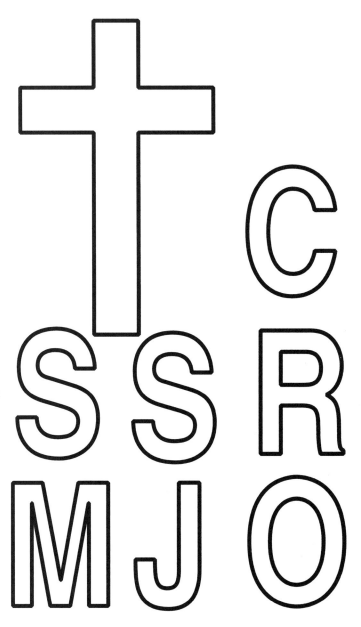

**JUDAS**

# Jesus' Love Reminder

## What You Need

- duplicated page and page 58
- brown and red construction paper
- 6" x 9" poster board
- hole punch
- glue
- yarn
- scissors
- tape

## What to Do

1. Copy the cross on brown construction paper and the heart on red construction paper for each child.
2. Instruct the students to cut out the cross and punch holes where indicated.
3. Allow the students to cut out the heart. Have them glue the heart on the left side of the poster board.
4. Instruct the students to tape one end of a length of yarn to the bottom back of the cross.
5. Show how to stitch the yarn back and forth through the cross to the top. They may tape the end on the back.

### What to Do, *continued*

6. Allow the students to glue the cross to the poster board to the right of the heart, overlapping it slightly.
7. Show where to punch holes at the top of the poster board. Help the children thread yarn through the holes for a hanger and tie the ends together.

**JUDAS**

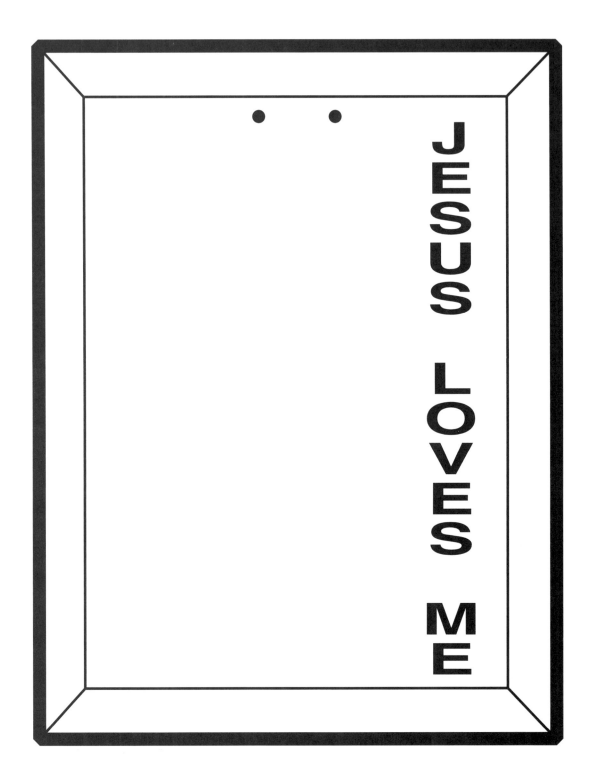

JESUS LOVES ME

# Judas, Lover of ?

On this worksheet you will find some scrambled words. These are things you could find in your mother's wallet. Unscramble the words, then place the circled letters on the lines to find out what Judas loved more than Jesus.

MIDE      __ __ Ⓞ __

ODALLR      __ Ⓞ __ __ __ __

LICEKN      Ⓞ __ __ __ __ __

UEQARTR      __ __ __ __ __ Ⓞ __

NENPY      __ __ __ Ⓞ __

Judas loved __ __ __ __ __ more than Jesus.

**What You Need**
• duplicated page
• pencils

**What to Do**
1. Give each child a duplicated page and a pencil.
2. Read the instructions aloud. Help students who have difficulty.
3. The answers are on page 93.

**JUDAS**

59

# craft/song

## What You Need
- duplicated page
- craft sticks
- crayons
- glue

## What to Do
1. Allow the children to color and cut out the coins.
2. Show how to fold each coin on the dashed line and glue a craft stick between the two sides.
3. Sing the song to the tune of "London Bridge," instructing the children to hold up the correct money stick as you sing.

# Money Was Best

Judas loved his money best,       (hold up #1)
Money best, money best.
Judas loved his money best.
More than the Lord.

Judas sold Jesus Christ,       (hold up frowning face)
Jesus Christ, Jesus Christ.
Judas sold Jesus Christ.
How very sad!

What do you love more than God?       (hold up question mark)
More than God, more than God?
What do you love more than God?
What do you love?

# Sandwich Coins

_____,
## lover of God – not money!
### 1 Timothy 6:10

_____,
## lover of God – not money!
### 1 Timothy 6:10

## craft/snack

### What You Need
- plastic sandwich bags
- hole punch
- yarn
- duplicated page
- bread, crusts removed
- soft cream cheese
- cheese strips
- knife
- rolling pin
- waxed paper

### What to Do
1. Cut the yarn into 18" lengths.
2. Show how to punch holes at 1" intervals around the bag's edge.
3. Have the children thread yarn through the holes.
4. Instruct the students to cut out the tag, write their name on it and tie it to their bag.
5. Give each student a waxed paper square and a piece of bread. Show how to roll the bread lightly with the rolling pin.
6. Allow the children to spread cream cheese on the bread.
7. Show how to lay a strip of cheese on one end of the bread and roll it up tightly.
8. Help the students cut the rolls into ½" coins. They may place the coins into the bag.

## JUDAS

## puzzle

### What You Need
• duplicated page
• red and yellow crayons

### What to Do
1. Give each child a duplicated page, a red crayon and a yellow crayon.
2. Read the instructions aloud. The answer is on page 93.

# Secret in the Coins

There is a secret in these coins. Color all of the 1¢ coins red and the 2¢ coins yellow. Fill in the blank below when you see the answer.

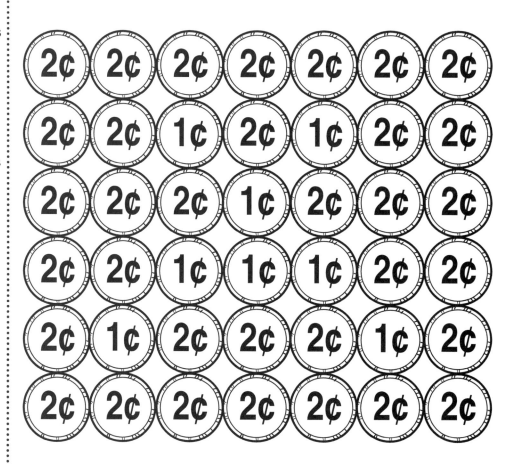

How did Judas feel when he sold Jesus for only 30 pieces of silver?

_____

**JUDAS**

# What Do You Sell Jesus For?

### What You Need
- white poster paper
- cross pattern
- stencil lettering
- brown paper
- old magazines
- yarn
- toy money
- scissors
- black marker

### What to Do
1. Cover the bulletin board with white poster paper.
2. Attach toy money around the board for a border.
3. Cut out and attach lettering to the top of the bulletin board as shown.
4. Write the memory verse at the bottom of the board.
5. Copy the cross on brown paper and attach it at the middle bottom of the board.
6. Cut out pictures of a car, toys which interest your class, clothes, etc.
7. Attach the pictures around the cross.
8. Connect the pictures to the cross with yarn.

**JUDAS**

63

## puzzle

### What You Need
- duplicated page
- crayons, two colors

### What to Do

1. Say, **Sometimes the wrong way is the easiest way, but the end is always sad when you go the wrong way. The right way may be harder now, but the reward is the greatest.**

2. Instruct the children to use one color of crayon to take the children the right way, and another color to take them the wrong way.

### What to Say

Judas was close to Jesus — one of His own disciples. You would think that he would have been extra good, but that is like saying, "Your dad is a pastor, so you'll get to heaven." Or, "You've gone to church your whole life — you must be a Christian." Just as Judas had a choice to do what was right or wrong, you have a choice, too. Judas chose the wrong way. What is your choice?

## JUDAS

# Your Own Salvation

REWARD

# Chapter 7
# Simon, the Disciple Who 'Got Along'

## 📖 Memory Verse

*He who loves a quarrel loves sin; he who builds a high gate invites destruction.* Proverbs 17:19

## 📖 Story to Share
## I Hate Tax Collectors

Simon was a zealot, full of zeal and enthusiasm. He hated tax collectors. He belonged to a group that rose up in protest against the Romans and their tax collectors.

When Jesus called Simon to be a disciple, Simon eagerly agreed to follow Him. He had watched Jesus perform miracles and had listened to His teachings. In his heart, Simon knew Jesus was God's Son.

Imagine Simon's surprise when he found a tax collector among the group of men who were to be Jesus' disciples!

*Matthew, a tax collector?* Simon said to himself. *Jesus has a tax collector among His disciples?*

Simon could feel Matthew's eyes on him as well. *He's probably wondering the same thing about me,* he thought. *Matthew probably wonders how Jesus could have a zealot among His closest friends.*

Simon didn't know what to do. He hated the tax collectors but he loved Jesus. Was his love for Jesus greater than his hatred? His heart told him Jesus wouldn't be pleased with hatred.

Then Simon heard Jesus talking to the group. "You are all important to Me — so important that I know how many hairs you have on your head. I know every small sparrow that falls to the ground, so you do not need to fear. You are more important than the sparrows."

Simon's eyes filled with happy tears as he realized how important he was to Jesus. Then a quick thought came to him: *Matthew is just as important to Jesus as I am.*

Simon nodded his head. He looked over at Matthew and met his eyes. With love in his heart, Simon smiled, feeling joyful when Matthew returned his smile. *This is okay,* he thought. *We'll get along.*

— based on Matthew 10:29-31

## ❓ Discussion Questions

1. What did Simon decide to do with Matthew? (get along)
2. Is there someone with whom you need to decide to get along?
3. Who can help you get along with those who are different from you? (Jesus)

### What You Need
- duplicated page
- crayons

### What to Do
1. Give each child a duplicated page and a crayon.
2. Read the instructions aloud. Help those who have difficulty.
3. To make the puzzle more fun, instruct the class that the first student to find all 10 smiles must stand up and say, "I'm smiling."

# Hidden Smiles

Find the 10 hidden smiles in the picture, then color the picture.

# I'll Get Along

**Teacher:** Students, I know your are just as excited about this guest as I am. Simon, we're so happy to have you here.

**Simon:** I'm glad to be here. As your teacher said, I am Simon. I am one of Jesus' disciples. Jesus is the Son of God. With my own eyes I have watched Jesus take five loaves of bread and two small fish and feed over 5,000 people. And He didn't just feed the people. There were 12 baskets full when the crowd finished eating. I saw Jesus make blind eyes see again, lame feet walk again and dead people live again.

But when I made the decision to be a disciple I didn't know that Jesus would pick tax collectors to be disciples, too. I hate tax collectors! In my culture, tax collecting is a dishonest profession. Tax collectors love money more than their country.

One day, Jesus told us, "You are all important to me — so important that I know how many hairs you have on your head." For some people, hairs on the head would not be hard to count, but I happen to have a full head of hair. Then I saw Matthew. He has even more hair than I do, yet Jesus knows how many hairs are there. That's how much He loves him.

That's when I said to myself, Simon, you've got to get along with Matthew. Jesus loves him as much as He loves you. It's a funny thing, you know. When I decided to get along with Matthew, I started to love that guy. So why don't you try it? It will work for you, too!

**Teacher:** Thank you, Simon. (turn to class) Is there someone with whom you have trouble getting along? I hope you try what Simon did. Remember, Jesus loves everyone!

## What You Need
- duplicated page
- robe with belt tie
- sandals
- towel

## What to Do
1. Choose a child who can read well to perform the monologue.
2. Instruct him or her to be expressive. Read it through together first. Wrap the performer's head in a towel like a turban.
3. Gather the children in a semi-circle and introduce your "guest."

**SIMON**

67

## craft

### What You Need
- duplicated page
- scissors
- glue
- construction paper

### What to Do

1. Instruct the students to think of a quarrel they have had with a friend that is still between them like "a high gate."
2. Allow the children to cut out the gate and the Scripture.
3. Show how to glue the verse to the construction paper, then the gate pieces to either side of the verse, so the gate will open to expose the verse.
4. Say, **If you have a closed gate between someone and yourself, take this paper to him or her and ask if the two of you can open the gate and be friends again.**

### What to Say

What happens when you quarrel with a friend? It's as if a high gate is between you and the friendship you shared with that friend — a gate that is closed.

### SIMON

# Inviting Destruction

He who loves a quarrel loves sin;
he who builds a high gate
invites destruction.

Proverbs 17:19

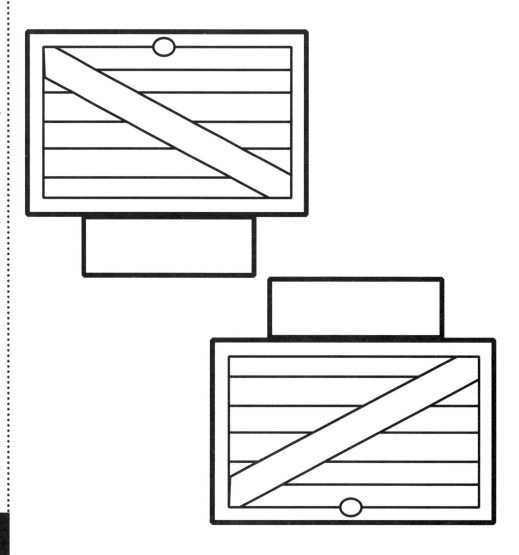

# My Theme

Simon, Simon, I've been thinking,
How can I be just like you?
I would like to be on your team,
Making get along my theme.

_____, _____,
I've been thinking.
How you could be just like me.
I want you to be on my team,
Making get along your theme.

He who loves a quarrel loves sin;
he who builds a high gate
invites destruction.

Proverbs 17:19

## craft/song

### What You Need
- duplicated page
- scissors
- tape

### What to Do
1. Allow the students to cut out the arm band.
2. Assist in taping a band around each child's arm.
3. Sing the song to the tune of "Reuben, Reuben," substituting a student's name for the second verse.
4. This song may also be used as a game, similar to "The Farmer In The Dell." Choose a child to be Simon, who stands in the middle while the others are in a circle walking around him and singing the first verse. Simon should choose one person from the circle, then have the group sing the second verse. Simon should then choose another, continuing until all are in the circle.

**SIMON**

### What You Need
- duplicated page
- red paper
- two-sided tape
- blindfold

### What to Do
1. Cut out and tape Simon to a wall at a height easily reached by your students.
2. Copy several smiles on red paper and cut them out, one per child.
3. Give each child a smile with tape on the back and instruct the students to write their name on it.
4. Blindfold each child, one at a time. Allow the student to stick the smile where he or she thinks it should go. As the child sticks the smile, he or she should pledge, "I will get along with others." The one closest to the correct spot is the winner.
5. The children can make a game to take home, so make sure you have extra Simons and smiles.

**SIMON**

# Pin the Smile

# Simon the Canaanite

*He who loves a quarrel loves sin;*
*he who builds a high gate invites destruction.*
**Proverbs 17:19**

My
name is

_____

Do you know someone who has the same name as yours? Maybe it is your father, so people call you "Junior." Or perhaps they add your last name or a nickname when speaking to you so you know which person to whom they are talking. Jesus had two disciples by the name of Simon. Jesus called one "Simon Peter" (or just "Peter"), and the other "Simon the Canaanite."

## craft

**What You Need**
- duplicated page
- magazine or newspapers
- glue
- scissors

**What to Do**
1. Instruct the students to cut out the name plate.
2. Show how to find the letters of their names in newspapers or magazines.
3. Instruct the students to cut out the letters and glue them to their name plate. They should find as many letters as possible, covering the bottom half of the name plate. The students may use their first name, full name or a nickname.
4. Show how to fold the name plate in half to stand.

**SIMON**

71

## puzzle

**What You Need**

- duplicated page
- pencils
- NIV Bibles

**What to Do**

1. Say, **Today you are going to do a puzzle to find out which disciple we are going to learn about. The first one finished should stand and say, "The disciple is _____."**

2. Hand out the puzzles, placing them face down on the table in front of the students. Instruct the students to turn to Luke 6:12-16.

3. At the "go" signal, the students should turn their papers over and complete the puzzle.

4. The answer is on page 93.

**SIMON**

# Today's Disciple

_____        verse 12, 4th word, 4th letter

_____        verse 13, 6th word, 2nd letter

_____        verse 14, 2nd word, 4th letter

_____        verse 15, 5th word, 1st letter

_____        verse 16, 2nd word, 3rd letter

Today's disciple is _____

# Tweety-Good

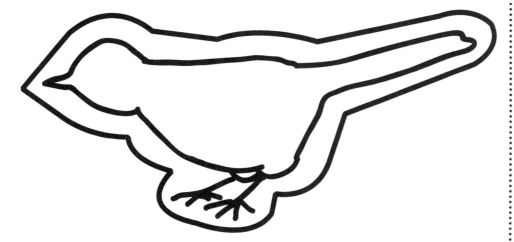

## snack

### What You Need
- duplicated page
- lunch meat
- celery leaves
- plastic knives
- sliced black olives

### What to Do
1. Give each child a slice of meat and a plastic knife.
2. Instruct the students to lay the sparrow pattern on the meat and cut around it to make a sparrow shape.
3. Show how to lay the celery leaf on the bird to look like a wing.
4. Demonstrate how to add a black olive eye.
5. Eat and enjoy!

**SIMON**

# Chapter 8
# Thomas, the Loyal Disciple

## Memory Verse

*Blessed is the man who perseveres under trial…he will receive the crown of life.* James 1:12

## Story to Share
## I'll Die With You

Jesus had a special friend named Lazarus. Lazarus' sisters were also Jesus' friends. One sister, Mary, showed her love for Jesus by anointing Him with a costly perfume and wiping His feet with her hair.

One day, word came to Jesus from the sisters. "Jesus, the one You love is sick. Please come so You can save his life."

Jesus gathered His disciples together. "I need to go to Bethany. Lazarus is sick."

The disciples immediately protested. "No, Jesus, it's not safe for You to go to Bethany."

"That's right," said James. "Remember the last time You were there?"

"I remember," said Philip. "The religious leaders tried to stone You, Jesus. You can't go back there."

"Yes, " agreed Matthew. "They'll try to kill us, too."

"I need to go," said Jesus firmly.

Thomas spoke up. "What does it matter what the danger is? We shouldn't hinder Jesus from doing His great work. Let's all go and, if need be, we will die with Him."

When the disciples reached Lazarus' home, they learned that Lazarus had already died. His body had been washed and placed in a linen cloth. A linen square was wrapped around his head. Those preparing Lazarus for burial had placed aloes and myrrh between the folds of the linen.

"Oh, Jesus," cried Martha. "If only You had been here, Lazarus would not have died."

They led Jesus to the tomb where Lazarus was laid. "Take away the stone," commanded Jesus. When the stone had been removed, Jesus said, "Lazarus, arise!"

At Jesus' call, Lazarus rose and walked toward Him. Thomas smiled. He was glad he had come. How he loved Jesus! He would be willing to be killed with Jesus, but he was thankful he was able to see this great miracle of the Lord.

— based on John 11

## Discussion Questions

1. How did Thomas show his loyalty to Jesus?

   (He was willing to travel to Bethany with Him even if it meant his death.)

2. What great miracle did Thomas witness because of his loyalty?

   (the raising of Lazarus from the dead)

# Crossword Verse

Fit the words from the memory verse in the squares below.

## Word List

| | | | |
|---|---|---|---|
| perseveres | blessed | trial | life |
| receive | is | he | of |
| crown | who | under | the |

Now write the verse on the lines below.

_____

_____

_____

puzzle
. . . . . . . . . . .

### What You Need
• duplicated page
• pencils

### What to Do
1. Give each child a duplicated page and a pencil.
2. Read the instructions aloud. Help those who have difficulty.
3. The answer key is on page 94.

**THOMAS**

75

## snack

### What You Need

- duplicated page
- hot plate
- large marshmallows
- baking chocolate
- candy sprinkles
- plastic drinking straws
- wax paper
- scissors

### What to Do

1. Cut out a tag for each child and cut the slit marks.
2. Place the chocolate in a bowl on a hot plate and allow it to melt. Note: Do not leave the hot plate unattended.
3. Give each child a square of waxed paper, two marshmallows and two straws.
4. Instruct the children to poke the marshmallows onto the straws.
5. Assist in dipping the marshmallow into the chocolate and then sprinkling with candy sprinkles.
6. Show how to the hold the straws together and slide them into the slit on the crown then slide it down.

**THOMAS**

# Excited Eyes

# Eyewitness News

## Cast

Reporter

Thomas

Lazarus

**Reporter:** So that just about wraps up the Bethany news for today, folks…

**Thomas:** Reporter, reporter, I saw it, I saw it!

**Reporter:** Excuse me?

**Thomas:** I saw it, reporter. Hurry and you can see it, too.

**Reporter:** Uh, folks, I guess there's more, although I don't know more of what. Where are you taking me, sir?

**Thomas:** To see it, reporter. I'm taking you to see it.

**Reporter:** Yes, follow along people, we're going to see it. Sir? What exactly is "it"?

**Thomas:** What I'm taking you to see, reporter.

**Reporter:** But what are you taking me to see? Oh, a ghost!

**Lazarus:** (wrapped in sheets or gauze) I'm alive! I'm alive.

**Thomas:** It's not a ghost — it's Lazarus, raised from the dead by Jesus. I saw it happen!

**Reporter:** Well, folks, I'd like to report something I've seen with my own eyes…

## skit

### What You Need
- duplicated page
- white sheets or gauze

### What to Do
1. Select three students for the roles. Give a copy of the script to just those three.
2. Wrap the student playing Lazarus in a white sheet or gauze.
3. You might want to repeat the skit to allow other students to participate.

**THOMAS**

# I Saw It Happen!

## craft

### What You Need
- duplicated page
- colored poster board
- scissors
- glue
- glitter

### What to Do
1. Have the students cut out the glasses pattern and trace it on poster board, then cut that out.
2. Help the students cut out the centers of the glasses.
3. Show how to spread glue on the glasses and sprinkle them with glitter.
4. Sing the song to the tune of "Deep and Wide," holding the glasses to your eyes at "I saw."

## I Saw Him!

I saw Him, I saw Him,
I saw Him raise Lazarus from the dead.
I saw Him, I saw Him,
I saw Him raise Lazarus from the dead.

Who did you see?    Yell: Jesus!
Who?    Yell: Jesus!
Who?    Yell: JESUS!!!

**THOMAS**

# Loyal Thomas and Happy Lazarus

## craft

### What You Need
- duplicated page
- crayons
- toilet tissue
- glue
- wiggle eyes
- scissors

### What to Do
1. Have the students cut out the Thomas and Lazarus figure.
2. Instruct the children to color Thomas.
3. Show how to wrap Lazarus in toilet tissue and glue it in place.
4. Allow the students to glue the wiggle eyes in place on both men.

**THOMAS**

# My Pledge of Loyalty

**craft**

## What You Need
- duplicated page
- ink stamp pad
- disposable hand wipes
- colored poster board
- scissors
- glue

## What to Do
1. Have the students cut out the pledge.
2. Help them cut a piece of poster board about 1" larger than the pledge all the way around.
3. Instruct the children to glue the pledge to the poster board.
4. Show how to press a thumb on the stamp pad and press it into the seal.
5. Help the students clean their hands with disposable wipes.

THOMAS

I,
Do solemnly pledge to remain
**LOYAL**
To Jesus Christ

Signature

Date

# True or False?

Some of the statements below are true and some are false. Circle the letter under the correct one. When you are finished, write the letters on the lines below to find a good character trait.

|  | TRUE | FALSE |
|---|---|---|
| 1. Jesus had a special friend named Lazarus. | L | B |
| 2. His sisters Mary and Esther loved Jesus, too. | R | O |
| 3. Lazarus broke his leg. | E | Y |
| 4. Lazarus lived in Bethany. | A | L |
| 5. The religious leaders in Bethany tried to poison Jesus. | F | L |
| 6. Thomas was willing to die for Jesus. | T | C |
| 7. Jesus brought Lazarus back to life. | Y | W |

___ ___  ___ ___ ___ ___ ___ ___  ___

**THOMAS**

81

### What You Need
- duplicated page
- crayons

### What to Do
1. Give each child a duplicated page and some crayons.
2. Read the instructions aloud.

### What to Say
Thomas' name means "a twin." No one knows for certain who Thomas' twin was. Some suggest that it might have been Matthew. Others think his twin was a woman named Lydia. In spite of the closeness twins feel to each other, Thomas was loyal to the one he loved best: Jesus.

# Twins

Can you find 10 pairs of twins in this picture? Color each pair a different color.

# More Disciple Activities

Duplicate this chart and hang one on the wall for each student. Lay each child's chart on the table each week. As the students come to class, encourage them to color the disciple for that week.

## JESUS' 12 DISCIPLES

| Peter | Matthew | Philip |
|-------|---------|--------|
| John | Andrew | Thomas |
| Simon | James | James |
| Judas | Bartholomew | Thaddaeus |

Name: _____

## craft

### What You Need
- duplicated page
- yellow paper
- glitter pen
- glue
- scissors
- cotton balls

### What to Do
1. Allow the children to cut out the heart and heaven.
2. Instruct the children to glue the heart to the bottom of heaven.
3. Show how to pull the cotton balls apart and place them around the top of the heart.
4. Allow the children to trace heaven with a glitter pen and allow it to dry.

### What to Say
We don't know much about this disciple of Jesus, but he was a true-blue disciple — his heart was pure. One day when Jesus was giving a sermon, He said, "Blessed are the pure in heart, for they will see God." (Matthew 5:8) Is your heart pure, like Bartholomew's?

**MORE DISCIPLE ACTIVITIES**

# Bartholomew, a True Blue Disciple

# James, the Disciple Who Prayed

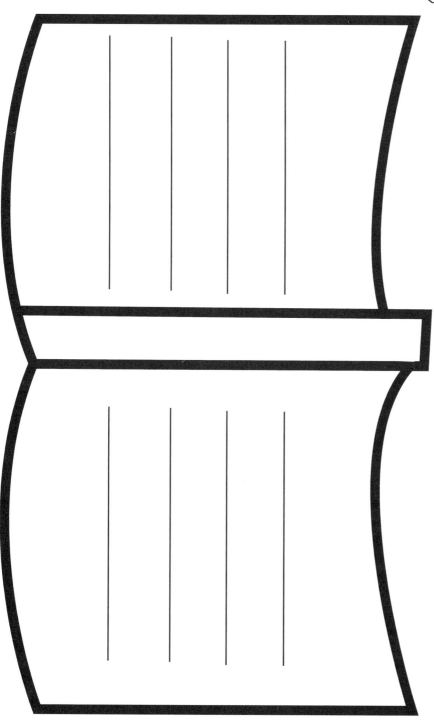

## craft

### What You Need
- duplicated page
- scissors
- glue
- Bibles
- pens
- ribbon

### What to Do
1. Have the students cut out the Bible and hands.
2. They should look up The Lord's Prayer in the Bible (Matthew 6:5-13) and write it on the lines of the Bible.
3. Show how to glue the ribbon down the middle of the Bible, then glue the hands on the end of the ribbon.

### What to Say
Jesus' disciples wanted to know how to pray. "Jesus, can You teach us?" they asked. Jesus gave them a pattern for prayer in Matthew 6:5-13. Do you know what we call this prayer? (The Lord's Prayer)

**MORE DISCIPLE ACTIVITIES**

# Philip, the Disciple with the Gift of Friendship

### What You Need
- duplicated page
- crayons

### What to Do
1. Give each child a duplicated page.
2. Read the story together and allow the students to replace the pictures with words.
3. Allow time for the students to draw a picture below the story.

### What to Say
Philip was a Galilean from Bethsaida of Galilee. He had a great gift for friendship. He served and loved Jesus, but had a special friendship with Andrew and Bartholomew. In order to have special friends you must love at all times (Proverbs 17:17). Philip knew that secret!

Read this story by replacing the pictures with words:

There was a little [picture] named Nancy. She had a special friend named Dustin. 1 day, Dustin fell and broke his [picture]. Nancy felt like [picture]. She got out her [picture] and a big piece of [picture]. Nancy folded the [picture] in ½. She drew ½ a [picture]. Then she got her [picture] and cut on the -------- she drew. When Nancy opened the [picture] it was a [picture] ! Nancy used a red [picture] and wrote, [picture] am sorry you broke your [picture]. I will [picture] for U. Nancy put the [picture] in an [picture] and mailed it 2 her friend. What can U do to make a friend [picture] ? Draw a picture of it below.

# Thaddaeus, the Disciple of the Heart

## craft

I'M A HEART
CHILD OF JESUS

### What You Need
- duplicated page
- poster board
- sequins
- glue
- magnets
- scissors

### What to Do
1. Duplicate the frame on poster board for each child.
2. Allow the students to cut out the frame. Assist in cutting out the inside oval.
3. Show how to glue sequins to the front of the frame, completely covering it.
4. Show how to glue the front to the back, gluing the sides and bottom of the frame and leaving the top open.
5. Allow the students to glue a magnet to the back. Encourage the students to insert a picture of themselves when they get home.

### What To Say

Thaddaeus was the disciple that had three names. Matthew called him "Lebbaeus, whose surname [last name] is Thaddaeus." Mark called him "Thaddaeus." Luke called him "Judas of James." The name "Lebbaeus" means "heart-child" in the Greek language. Thaddaeus was one of the youngest disciples and he was looked upon with affection by the older men. The disciples gave him nicknames to show their love. You, too, are a "heart-child." Jesus loves you and calls you "My child."

## MORE DISCIPLE ACTIVITIES

## puzzle

### What You Need
• duplicated page
• colored paper
• pencils

### What to Do
1. Duplicate the bookmark separately from the puzzle on colored paper and cut one out for each child.
2. Instruct the students to find the names of all of the disciples in the puzzle.
3. If the students have difficulty remembering the names of the disciples, hand out the bookmarks.
4. The answer key is on page 95.

**MORE DISCIPLE ACTIVITIES**

# Name Those Twelve

```
K R J M L E B B D B S V C C
J S S O W E R D N A A P M N
A E I V B X H J Q S M E M C
M M M L H C U W V E O T T Q
E A O J K X K J Y E H E K T
S J N W E M O L O H T R A B
W Q J P E W M A T T H E W K
J S Z I L N B O W S G D C R
U U R L I H A S G D K L Q I
D Z G I T O H G M Q D K E C
A S I H U J A M E S J B W J
S R H P S S U E A D D A H T
```

## Jesus' Twelve Disciples

**Peter**
**Andrew**
**James**
**John**
**Philip**
**Thomas**
**Matthew**
**James**
**Thaddaeus**
**Simon**
**Judas**
**Bartholomew**

# Disciple Day

---

**What: A Disciple Day**

**When:** _____

**Where:** _____

Come dressed like one of the disciples and let us guess who you are.

By this all men shall know that you are my disciples, If you love one another.
John 13:5

Prize given if you know the memory verse when you come!

---

### What You Need
- duplicated page and page 90
- parchment paper
- yarn
- glue
- spring-type clothespins
- markers
- certificate, p. 91
- mesh bags
- candy coins

### What to Do
1. Plan this event for the Sunday after you complete this unit on Jesus' Disciples.
2. Copy the invitation on parchment paper and cut it out. Roll it scroll-like and tie with yarn. Give one to each child the Sunday prior to the event. (Costume ideas to try: bathrobes and turbans; Judas carrying a coin bag; Peter carrying a rock; John pinning a heart on himself.)
3. Copy the name tags and cut them out. Glue each tag to a clothespin.

## What to Do, continued
4. Give each student a name tag and write his or her Bible name on the tag. Instruct the students to call each other by their Bible names.
5. Play the game from the unit that was your students' favorite.
6. Talk about which disciple was each student's favorite and why.
7. Have a ceremony to hand out the "Yippee for Me" certificates on page 91.
8. Give each child a small mesh bag of candy coins as he or she leaves.

**MORE DISCIPLE ACTIVITIES**

**I'm a
disciple of
Jesus!**

_____

**I'm a
disciple of
Jesus!**

_____

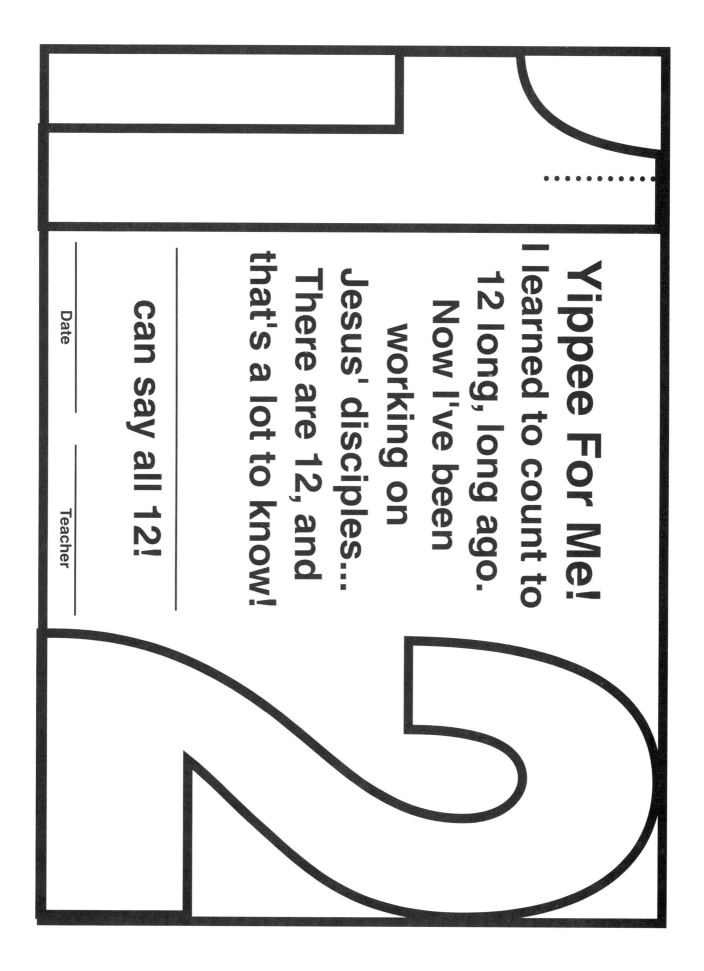

# Yippee For Me!

I learned to count to
12 long, long ago.
Now I've been
working on
Jesus' disciples...
There are 12, and
that's a lot to know!

_____ can say all 12!

_____  _____
Date                    Teacher

# Answer Key

## ANDREW
*Back and Forth*, p. 8

*Here, Jesus*, p. 10
Sea of Galilee, followed, eight, bite, boy, five, two, thanks, twelve

## JAMES
*Full of Zeal*, p. 18
It is fine to be zealous, provided the purpose is good. Galatians 4:18

## JOHN
*Who Showed Love?*, p. 36
Abraham, David and Jonathan, Elisha, wise men, Jesus, Mary, Samaritan, God

## PETER
*Following Peter's Example*, p. 38
Simon Peter answered, "You are the Christ, the Son of the living God." Matthew 16:16

*Peter's Name*, p. 42
fisherman
Simon
Cephas
walk
rock

*Precious Peter*, p. 45
Faith
Blood
Cornerstone
Promises

## MATTHEW
*Leaving It All*, p. 49
Eternal Life

*Tax Collector Matthew*, p. 53
talents
gold, silver, copper
The love of money is the root of all kinds of evil.
love

## JUDAS
*Judas, Lover of ?*, p. 59
dime, dollar, nickel, quarter, penny, money

*Secret in the Coins*, p. 62

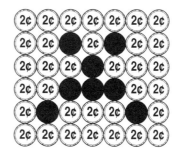

## SIMON
*Today's Disciple*, p. 72
SIMON

## THOMAS

*Crossword Verse*, p. 75

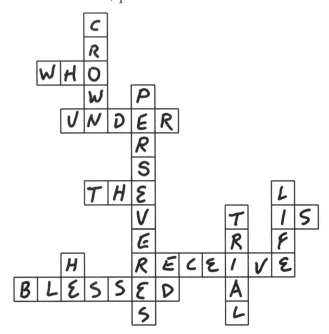

*True or False*, p. 81
LOYALTY

## MATTHEW

*Hidden Verse*, p. 49

# MORE DISCIPLE ACTIVITIES

*Name Those Twelve*, p. 88

```
K R J M L E B B D B S V C C
J S S O W E R D N A A P M N
A E I V B X H J Q S M E M C
M M L H C U W V E O T T Q
E A O J K X K J Y E H E K T
S J N W E M O L O H T R A B
W Q J P E W M A T T H E W K
J S Z I L N B O W S G D C R
U U R L I H A S G D K L Q I
D Z G I T O H G M Q D K E C
A S I H U J A M E S J B W J
S R H P S S U E A D D A H T
```